How to Train Your Australian Shepherd

A Complete Guide to Obedience, Socialization, and Behavior Modification Training for Aussies

Finnley Crestwood

Disclaimer

The information in this book is intended for general guidance on training. It is not a substitute for professional advice. Always consult with a veterinarian or certified dog trainer for tailored recommendations. The author and publisher disclaim any liability for actions taken based on the content of this book.

How to Train your
Australian Shepherd

BONUS:
20 Australian Shepherd Homemade Food Recipes

A Complete Guide to Obedience, Socialization, and Behavior Modification Training for Aussies

Contents

Introduction   7

Chapter One   11

Understanding the Australian Shepherd   11

Origins and History of the Breed   11

Typical Temperament and Personality Traits   13

Physical Characteristics and Attributes   14

Chapter Two   17

Preparing for Your Australian Shepherd Puppy   17

Gathering Essential Supplies for Puppyhood   17

Puppy-Proofing Your Home   20

Finding a Reputable Breeder or Rescue   23

Chapter Three   27

Bringing Home Your Australian Shepherd Puppy   27

Preparing for the First 24 Hours   27

House-Training 101   30

Crate Training Fundamentals   32

Chapter Four   **35**

Socializing Your Australian Shepherd Puppy

35

Importance of Early Socialization   35

Introducing Your Puppy to New Places   37

Getting Your Puppy Used to Handling   40

Chapter Five   **43**

Training a Young Australian Shepherd   **43**

Beginning Obedience Commands   43

Clicker Training Methods   45

Why Clicker Train   46

Preventing Nipping and Biting   48

Chapter Six   **51**

Advanced Training Techniques   **51**

Expanding Commands and Cues   51

Off-Leash Control   53

Agility and Trick Training   56

Chapter Seven   **59**

Common Behavioral Issues   **59**

Separation Anxiety   59

Excessive Barking/Herding   62

Digging/Chewing Destructiveness   65

Chapter Eight   **69**

Nutrition and Exercise Needs   **69**

Dietary Requirements for Aussies   69

Establishing Feed Schedules   72

Importance of Daily Exercise and Mental Stimulation   74

Chapter Nine   **79**

Grooming and Health Care   **79**

Brushing and Bathing Basics   79

Nail Trimming and Dental Care   82

Vaccination and Vet Visit Schedules   84

Chapter Ten   **87**

The Joys of Living with an Australian Shepherd   **87**

Enjoying Your Fully-Trained Aussie   87

Competing in Dog Sports   89

Traveling and Adventuring with Your Dog   91

Special bonus   **95**

20 homemade food dish ideas for Australian Shepherds with ingredients and preparation instructions   95

Introduction

Among all dog breeds, the Australian Shepherd ranks high in intelligence, energy, and trainability. This kind of herding dog has always appealed to me because of my childhood spent on a ranch with working dogs. They are intelligent, adaptable, and driven. Consequently, an Australian Shepherd was a no-brainer for me as a new family pet following my wedding. I was aware, too, that bringing a puppy of such an energetic and independent breed into the world would necessitate early and consistent training if I wanted to channel its boundless energy into a well-behaved companion.

Return to the day when I took Tango home as a cute little eight-week-old puppy. I could tell I was in for a wild trip the second those brilliant blue eyes met mine. In spite of his eagerness to please and rapid command acquisition, Tango's energetic personality necessitated continual stimulation and close supervision during his formative months. He was typical of Australian dogs in that he would bite, herd his toys, and push boundaries until I gave him something to do with all that boundless energy.

We had to take a crash course in the specific requirements of this intelligent breed in order to provide the groundwork for training that would ensure our survival and prosperity. Dragging my fatigued self out of bed at dawn for brisk morning walks before work, scattering toys to be "herded" into bins, signing up for fitness courses, researching mental puzzles - no activity or game was off limits if it engaged Tango's body and mind. This breed is so dedicated to its job that I soon realized that a weary puppy is a well-behaved dog.

Now, I won't pretend that teaching Tango home manners, impulse control, and fundamental cues was a walk in the park every day. We endured our fair share of chewed-up shoes, demand barking, and counter-surfing antics from his keen nose. But by knowing what fulfills an Australian Shepherd's instincts and changing my training approach accordingly, Tango's mischievous habits steadily evolved into rock-solid obedience.

Today, I'm rewarded with an attentive hiking partner who stays close off-leash, a teammate who lives to run agility courses at my side, and a trustworthy best friend who respects limits in the home. Was it an intensive road getting here? Absolutely. But the payoff of living with a well-rounded Australian Shepherd is immeasurable.

This leads me to the book you now possess - a complete roadmap to training based on my direct experience with this smart, strong-willed breed. Consider me your buddy; I've made all the mistakes and can lead you to the shortcuts! Whether you're struggling through the puppy phase or need advice pushing your Aussie's talents to the next level, this guide will empower you to completely enjoy life with your Australian Shepherd in a good, knowledgeable way. When you give the time and energy this rare breed deserves, you'll be rewarded with a dedicated companion for adventures, activities, and life's ordinary joys.

So let's get started changing that headstrong ball of Australian Shepherd hair into your ideal canine buddy! I'm convinced the stages in this book will help you acquire insight, develop leadership, and cultivate an exceptional friendship with your beloved Aussie. Just don't be surprised when your neighbors start asking for training ideas after observing your dog's newfound manners and abilities - we'll be an inspiration together! Now let's go on this voyage.

Chapter One

Understanding the Australian Shepherd

Origins and History of the Breed

The Australian Shepherd has relatively unknown origins despite its moniker. The breed was not developed in Australia at all. Most breed historians believe the origins of the Aussie were herding dogs brought to the United States by Basque shepherds going through Australia in the 1800s. These hardy herding dogs were crossed with other European herding breeds while in the U.S. The moniker "Australian Shepherd" possibly stems from them being linked with Aussie sheepherders.

The Australian Shepherd became famous in the western U.S. as an all-purpose ranch dog due to their intelligence and strong work ethic. They excelled at herding livestock, especially sheep, cattle, and horses. Their middle size gave them an agility advantage against larger collateral herding breeds. The breed's popularity expanded in the 1950s and they were first registered with the American Kennel Club in 1957.

Today, the Australian Shepherd remains a valued and active herding breed. They are affiliated with rodeo and are frequently seen working cattle farms. Their intelligence and enthusiasm to work have made them outstanding service dogs, search and rescue dogs, and participants in canine sports like agility and flyball. The Australian Shepherd is also rising in popularity as an active family companion. They are the 15th most popular breed in the United States according to AKC registration figures.

Typical Temperament and Personality Traits

The Australian Shepherd is a clever, work-oriented, and energetic breed. They are loyal, dedicated companions that try to satisfy their owners. Aussies are easy to train since they appreciate having a job to accomplish. This is a highly clever breed that needs constant mental stimulation and exercise. Without suitable outlets for their energy and intelligence, these dogs are prone to developing behavioral difficulties including hyperactivity and destructive chewing.

Australian Shepherds are not lap dogs comfortable with sleeping on the couch all day. They flourish when given a job and room to run. This means they are better suited to active owners who can give them 30-60 minutes of vigorous exercise every day. Mental stimulation through training sessions, puzzle toys, and interactive play is also beneficial.

This is not a breed that can be left alone in the backyard. They need interaction with their people.

The typical Aussie attitude is loyal, intellectual, work-oriented, and vivacious. They are quick learners but can be independent thinkers. Aussies will get bored and destructive if under-stimulated. They build close ties with their owners and try to be helpful companions. This is a sensitive breed that does not respond well to severe reprimand or training methods. Kind, positive reinforcement brings out their eager-to-please character.

Physical Characteristics and Attributes

The Australian Shepherd is a medium-sized dog averaging 18-23 inches tall at the shoulder and weighing between 35-65 pounds. They are powerful, athletic herding dogs built for a long day's labor. The Aussie has a medium-length double coat that provides protection from the elements. The exterior coat is straight or wavy and weather-resistant. The undercoat is soft and dense.

Aussie coats come in a variety of startling colors such as pure black, red merle, blue merle, red tricolor, and red. Merle coats exhibit variegated spots of color and are a distinguishing marking. No two Australian Shepherds look precisely the same. The breed frequently has striking brown and white markings on the face, chest, legs, and bottom.

This is a moderately long-lived breed with an average lifespan of 12-15 years. Australian Shepherds are prone to health disorders such as hip dysplasia, eye difficulties, epilepsy, and autoimmune diseases. Reputable breeders will test breeding dogs for these concerns to generate healthy puppies.

Key physical features of the Aussie include:

- Medium-sized, athletic build
- Muscular and agile - Weather-resistant double coat - Variety of stunning coat colors and patterns
- Perky, upright ears
- Bobbed or docked tail - Intelligent, expressive eyes
- Fast, energetic gait

The Australian Shepherd's physical traits reflect its heritage and role as an agile, tireless herding dog able to keep up with sheep in tough terrain or harsh weather conditions. Their vitality and stamina are matched by a keen intellect and commitment that make Aussies the ultimate all-around ranch dog.

Chapter Two

Preparing for Your Australian Shepherd Puppy

Gathering Essential Supplies for Puppyhood

Preparing for the arrival of an Australian Shepherd puppy requires acquiring all the things needed for their health, safety, training, and enjoyment during the first months at home. Having the correct gear packed ahead of time makes the transition easy for both the pup and the owner. Here are some essentials to keep on hand:

Collar and Leash - An adjustable flat collar and 6-foot leash are needed for walks, tags, and lead training. Go with a limited-slip martingale collar to prevent escapes.

ID Tag - An ID tag with your contact info is necessary in case your pet gets loose. Include your name, cell phone, and address.

box - A wire box with a tray floor works nicely for an Aussie pup. Make sure it is sized adequately to provide enough room when fully grown. Crates instruct pups to contain their urine and provide them with a personal den.

Dog Bed - A luxurious, orthopedic bed will become your pup's favorite napping location. Place it in a corner of the bedroom or general living space.

Bowls - Durable stainless steel bowls won't harbor bacteria. Buy one for water and one for food. Consider a no-tip bowl.

Puppy Food - High-quality dry puppy food stimulates muscle growth and brain development. Pick a suitable large-breed puppy formula.

Treats - Soft puppy treats are perfect for initial training. Choose natural options with ingredients you recognize.

Toys - Interactive puzzle toys and rubber chew toys will save your possessions from sharp dog teeth. Rotate to keep it interesting.

Grooming Supplies - A slicker brush, undercoat rake, and nail clippers will help keep your Aussie's coat neat. Introduce grooming cautiously.

Cleaning Supplies – Stock up on paper towels, pet-safe cleansers, stain removers, etc. Accidents will happen during housetraining!

Baby Gates - Use gates to block off areas and keep your pup isolated in dog-proofed zones. They prevent chasing cats or youngsters.

The first few weeks are all about developing habits, bonding, and careful introductions. Having all the appropriate gear packed makes it easy to focus on training during this key socialization phase. Shop early so your Aussie puppy gets off to a wonderful start!

Puppy-Proofing Your Home

Before bringing home an Australian Shepherd puppy, take time to completely dog-proof your house and yard. Their curious curiosity and predilection for chewing means attentive prevention now will save you trouble later. Focus on removing dangers and safeguarding assets.

shut Access: Use baby gates to shut off rooms, stairs, and dangerous locations like kitchens and restrooms. Keep pups restricted to locations you can directly supervise.

Remove Hazards: Get rid of dangerous houseplants, hide exposed wires, secure unsteady furniture, and prevent little design objects from being swallowed.

Secure Trash: Use cans with locking lids or keep trash behind closed doors. Pups love tearing paper things and eating food scraps.

Keep Items Up High: Australian Shepherds are agile jumpers. Keep anything you don't want to be chewed up high on shelves or in closets. Watch counters too.

Hide Shoes and Clothes: Don't entice your puppy - put all shoes, slippers, socks, underwear, etc. away in closets with the doors shut.

Pick Up Stray Items: Do a sweep for any stray bits of paper, children's toys, remote controllers, etc. Anything is fair game for a teething Aussie!

Check for Gaps: Make sure low windows are securely closed. Block any potential escape spots or hiding areas. Confine to small spaces first.

Dog-Proof Yard: Fully fence in your yard - Aussies are great escape artists! Ensure hazardous plants are removed, waste secured, and fences dog-proof.

By thoroughly puppy-proofing ahead of time, you can relax knowing risks and valuables are out of reach. Reassess as your puppy grows for any new risks. Prevention is the greatest method to avoid damaging chewing tendencies in Australian Shepherds.

Finding a Reputable Breeder or Rescue

Acquiring an Australian Shepherd puppy should be done carefully to guarantee you acquire a healthy, sound representative of the breed from an ethical source. Whether going through a breeder or rescue, perform in-depth research to avoid supporting puppy mills or irresponsible methods.

Seeking a Breeder:

- Locate breeders via the Australian Shepherd Club of America who follow the club's ethical breeding guidelines.

- Make sure genetic health testing is done on parent dogs for concerns including Collie Eye Anomaly, hip dysplasia, and MDR1 medication sensitivity.

- Ask to see where pups are raised. Look for clean conditions, socializing, vet exams, and good care.

- Talk to references and ask about the breeder's techniques, experience, and how long dogs are kept.

- Good breeders focus on temperament, health, and breed preservation - not profit. Be aware of popular "designer" blends.

Finding a Rescue:

- Search for Australian Shepherd-specific rescues locally and nationwide to adopt.

- Ensure the rescue thoroughly vets dogs for health and temperament issues before adopting them out.

- Ask about any behavior assessments done. Know the dog's history if possible.

- Make sure a contract is in place requiring returning dogs if it doesn't work out. Avoid rehoming regularly.

- Rescues require volunteers informed about the Aussie breed. Ask to talk with one.

- Be realistic about your lifestyle and experience when choosing rescue pets.

Take your time investigating reliable options. Never purchase puppies from pet stores or hasty web adverts. Be selective to find the ideal Australian Shepherd for your home.

Chapter Three

Bringing Home Your Australian Shepherd Puppy

Preparing for the First 24 Hours

The first day and night home with your Australian Shepherd puppy builds the basis for their integration into your life. Take steps to make their adjustment as seamless, low-stress, and positive as possible. Be prepared to provide comfort combined with moderate guidance.

Puppy-Proof Again - Do double-check for risks and safeguard off-limit places. Confine to one or two puppy-safe spaces first.

Gather Supplies - Have food, snacks, a routine, collar, leash, bed, toys, pee pads, cleaners, etc. prepared and immediately available.

Pet-Proof Your Yard - Triple-check fencing, hide wires/tools, secure gates/sheds, remove plants. Don't take chances with an active and inquisitive Aussie puppy.

Establish A Routine - Set up designated feeding times, play sessions, training periods, walks, and created naps to start a predictable routine immediately.

Allow Decompression - The travel home is exhilarating and stressful. Allow lots of breaks for peaceful bonding and adjustment before introducing your dog to kids, other pets, etc.

Manage Interactions - Keep introductions to new people and animals brief and positive.

Overwhelming your puppy risks fear imprinting. Go slowly.

Capture Calm Moments - When your dog disengages to rest, softly praise and treat. Use these moments to bond and teach settling.

Accidents Happen! - Expect mishaps with toilet training and chewing. Respond softly - never punish. Manage the environment and redirect to relevant stuff.

Make It Positive - During the first 24 hours, focus on creating trust through affection, delectable snacks, engaging toys, and entertaining voice tones - avoid scolding.

Provide Love and Security - Australian Shepherd puppies bond intimately with their people. Meet their needs swiftly, respond to screams, and offer encouragement as they adjust.

The first day sets the tone for socializing an Australian Shepherd puppy. Go slow, troubleshoot issues, and keep things low-key and positive. Meeting their demands consistently will increase your pup's confidence.

House-Training 101

House-training an Australian Shepherd puppy demands attentive supervision, routine, positive reward, and rapid clean-up of any accidents. Patience and persistence are crucial during the 4-6 month period. Understand effective strategies to get your Aussie pup toilet trained.

Establish a Routine - Take your pooch out first thing in the morning, after naps, playtime, meals, and every 30-60 minutes while active. Puppies urinate regularly.

Choose a Potty site - Pick a specific site outside and always use this area. The odors awaken toilet impulses. Praise and provide treats when they go to the appropriate spot.

Use a Cue - Say a phrase like "go potty" when your pooch pees or poops so they associate the words with the action.

Supervise Constantly - Don't take your eyes off a young pup indoors as accidents happen rapidly. Keep them leashed for you if needed. Confine when you can't watch.

Reward Success - Cheer, give goodies, and offer pets when your pup completes pottying outside. This motivates them to hold it indoors next time.

Clean All Accidents - Use an enzymatic cleanser to completely remove scents that may entice your dog to urinate there again.

Avoid Scolding - If you find your pup in the act indoors, hastily yell "outside!" and swiftly take them to their potty spot. No punishment.

Prevent Accidents - Limit access, use a crate when you're occupied, and clean up water bowls at night. The more success your pet has, the quicker they learn.

Be Patient - Australian Shepherd puppies might take up to 6 months to be fully housetrained. Consistency, positive reinforcement, and management do the trick.

Crate Training Fundamentals

Properly crate training an Australian Shepherd puppy leverages their natural denning tendencies to create a safe personal place where they'll happily relax. Introduce crating gradually with positive connections to get your puppy comfortable using their crate regularly.

Select the Right Crate - It should give a standing area but not excessive space. Place it in a central living space during the day.

Make It Inviting - Add a nice bed, soft toys, and snacks. Feed your puppy in the open crate to generate happy feelings.

Take It Slow - Begin with brief sessions and lots of praise and rewards for freely entering. Never force them in.

Create Positive Associations - Randomly give treats and toys inside the crate so your pooch associates them with pleasant things happening.

Use as a Reward - When your puppy willingly enters, shout "Kennel up!" and reward it with a food treat. Make going in satisfying.

Feed Meals Inside - After introducing the crate, begin feeding your puppy all their meals inside their crate to reinforce it as a happy area.

Keep Sessions Brief - Start with just 10-15 minutes at a time with the door open as you supervise nearby. Slowly increase duration.

Puppy Nap Time - When your puppy gets tired/overstimulated, signal "kennel up" and offer them a chew toy while you leave them for a nap break.

Night Time - Place the crate in your bedroom at night. Aussies don't like to be entirely removed from their people.

Aussies catch on rapidly when crate training is a pleasurable experience. Patiently help your pup associate their kennel with food, sleep, praise, and protection.

Chapter Four

Socializing Your Australian Shepherd Puppy

Importance of Early Socialization

Socializing an Australian Shepherd puppy at the important developmental time between 3-16 weeks is vital to raising a confident, well-adjusted dog. Early favorable exposures to people, places, animals, textures, sounds, and handling prepare children for the world.

Prevents Fearfulness - Pups exposed to unusual objects before 12-14 weeks react with curiosity rather than dread when older. Their brains are conditioned to perceive novel stimuli as non-threatening while young.

Improves confidence - Frequent positive experiences in the puppy socialization window improve nerve strength and resilience. They learn how to approach new situations with a sense of confidence.

Teaches acceptable Behavior - Proper socialization includes teaching acceptable play behavior with other dogs, greeting manners with people, and keeping calm in exciting surroundings.

Increases Adaptability - A well-rounded foundation prepares an Aussie for everything ranging from bustling metropolitan living to active rural farm life. Early diversity creates flexibility.

Promotes Handling - Getting puppies accustomed to being touched, caressed, having feet/ears/mouth handled, and restrained prepares them for vet checkups, grooming, and injuries.

Avoids Potential hostility - Insufficient socialization during the puppy window can lead to fear-based hostility toward unknown people, animals, sounds, or settings later in life.

While socialization continues throughout life, the most essential developmental period finishes at 16 weeks. Prioritize safe, organized exposure to develop the strongest foundation during this prime puppy phase.

Introducing Your Puppy to New Places

An important component of socializing an Australian Shepherd puppy entails gradually introducing them to new places and surroundings.

Ensure these initial experiences are calm, controlled, and associated with lots of praise and treats.

Around Your Neighborhood - Let your pet meet neighborhood kids, dogs, people gardening, cars passing, cyclists, joggers, etc. Go during peaceful periods at first.

Pet-Friendly Stores - Bring your pup on short visits to home improvement stores, outdoor malls, farming supply shops, pet stores, outdoor cafés, etc.

Friends' Homes - Arrange playdates at households of friends/family who have vaccinated, gentle dogs and cats. Let your pooch get adjusted to changing homes.

Outdoor Areas - Explore parks, hiking paths, ponds and lakesides (carried), outdoor malls, beaches, green spaces like sports grounds, etc.

Handling Noises - Introduce car rides, doorbells, clapping, vacuums, crinkling bags, fallen pans, loud machinery like leaf blowers, etc.

Handled softly - Ask friends and family to approach, pet softly, and offer treats as you supervise body handling and mouth inspection.

Public Transportation - With cautious handling and a sling, acclimate your puppy to buses, trains, ferries, and waiting in stations when spacing allows.

Rest Stops - Stop at parking lots, rest areas, and lovely scenic outlooks during travels to let your dog explore on a leash.

Socialization settings can include anywhere in your region safe for a young puppy. Keep sessions quick and lively. Ensure your Aussie pooch keeps up-to-date on shots before public visits.

Getting Your Puppy Used to Handling

An Australian Shepherd that tolerates basic handling, grooming, medical treatment, and physical inspection makes ownership much easier. Use the puppy socialization time to get them acquainted with:

- Having paws, legs, and tails touched
- Ears inspected
- Mouth opened for tooth/gum inspection
- Being hugged/restrained/rolled over
- Being lifted and carried
- Having fur brushed
- Being bathed and dried
- Having nails clipped
- Vet examinations

Tips for Success:

- Handle frequently for brief moments from the first day home
- Pair with treats and praise to build positive feelings
- Gently restrain and get the puppy used to recovering freedom
- Touch toes, tail, ears, muzzle when the puppy is sleepy or eating
- Make grooming feel good by giving treats after and during
- Role play vet exams with fake thermometers, stethoscopes, restraint
- Seek assistance from groomers and vet staff to practice touching
- Keep experiences upbeat
- avoid scolding puppy if they resist
- Go carefully and give puppy pauses as required
- don't overwhelm

Daily short, positive handling ensures your Aussie puppy develops acceptance of contact, grooming, vet appointments, and essential handling as they mature. Always heed puppy discomfort cues and keep forceful handling to a minimum.

Chapter Five

Training a Young Australian Shepherd

Beginning Obedience Commands

Starting basic obedience early provides a foundation of respect and control with your Australian Shepherd puppy. Keep lessons cheerful and rewarding. Work on one cue at a time using goodies, praise, and consistency.

Sit - Hold a goodie above the pup's nose and slowly move it back between its ears coaxing it into a sit position, say "sit", praise, and reward. Practice until they associate the verbal cue with the action.

Down - Ask for a seat, hold the treat right in front of their nose, slowly lower the treat straight down to the floor during the pup into a down, say "down", and mark and treat when they follow.

Stay - After a sit, say "stay", take a step back, return, and reward if they held the stay. Gradually increase distance and duration. Change places too.

Come - Say the pup's name and "Come!" in an enthusiastic voice, run backward inviting them to follow for a treat reward. NEVER call to punish, always make coming pleasurable.

Leave It - Say "leave it", offer a treat in the palm of your hand, and cover with the other hand when pup licks or nibbles. Praise and reward only when they cease engaging with your hand.

Loose Leash Walking - Reward your dog for focusing on you and staying by your side. Change direction often. Stop when they pull and wait for the slack leash before proceeding again.

Use 5-10 minute sessions, positive reinforcement, patience, and inventiveness. End on successes, keep it entertaining! Fade rewards progressively once the notion is learned. Remember - a young Aussie puppy has an extremely limited attention span.

Clicker Training Methods

Clicker training uses a distinct "click" noise as a marker to precisely convey to your Australian Shepherd puppy the exact instant they execute the desired behavior. The click is promptly followed by a reward.

Charging the Clicker - First, pair the clicker sound with treats by clicking and delivering treats without asking for any behaviors. Do this repeatedly until the puppy looks expectantly for a treat upon hearing the click.

Adding the Cue - Next, say the behavior cue such as "sit" and when the dog sits, click followed immediately by a food reward. Repeat until the pup associates the cue + behavior with the click then treat.

Proof the Behavior - Once the pup reliably executes the cued behavior, practice in multiple situations, from distances, and with additional distractions. Keep rewarding successes.

Why Clicker Train

- The distinct click sounds clearly indicate the proper behavior against a spoken "good dog" which may be delayed, allowing the dog to miss what they did right.

- The click always predicts an upcoming reward, providing a strong reinforcement association and pushing the puppy to actively problem-solve what activities will earn a click.

- Clicker training increases skills through positive reinforcement vs addressing unwanted behaviors. Dogs learn faster when they are eager to figure out how to get rewards.

Tips for Effective Clicker Training:

- Keep sessions brief and upbeat, always ending on victories.

- Vary rewards - mix in toys, pets, play as well as food items to keep the puppy involved.

- Gradually phase off continuous clicking for well-known behaviors, utilizing intermittent variable reinforcement.

- Use precise cues, limit weak orders, and praise liberally for puppy-providing behaviors.

Clicker training meshes wonderfully with the clever, energetic temperament of the Australian Shepherd. The strategy keeps both owner and dog actively engaged in good learning moments.

Preventing Nipping and Biting

Since Australian Shepherd puppies are highly energetic herders, it's necessary to teach appropriate mouth manners early to prevent painful nipping or biting of hands, limbs, or clothing. Never let this behavior go unchallenged.

Understand the Cause - Pups may be overstimulated, teething, herding, or trying to initiate play. Nipping draws attention. Any pressure from teeth should be discouraged from the outset nevertheless.

Respond Properly - For light mouthing, deliver a high-pitched "ouch", and withdraw all attention for 15-30 seconds. Praise calm behavior when they stop.

Interrupt - For more committed grabbing/nipping, shout "No bite!", take their collar, and lead them to the timeout spot for 1-2 minutes till relaxed. Then redirect to a plush Kong or chew toy.

Prevent Rehearsal - Closely supervise play, greetings, and handling. Any time teeth touch skin - instant timeout with toy diversion. Do not allow bites.

Encourage Toys - Stuff a Kong or chew toy in the pup's mouth after interruptions to educate what they should chew on instead of hands or limbs. Always keep toys handy.

Avoid Rough Play - No grabbing jowls, wrestling, or play fighting. This might boost nibbling and arousal. Model nice pets and calm handling.

Phase Out Feeding from Hands - Make eating only from chew toys and puzzle feeders. Don't feed from hand or mouth nipping can escalate.

Say "Enough!" - If your pup gets too excited playing, firmly say "Enough!", get up and ignore. Wait for quiet before starting mild play.

With extremely young puppies, gentle supervision is crucial as biting inhibition is still developing. Harsh reprimands might make nipping and aggressiveness issues worse. Be patient and consistent - an Aussie pup will quickly follow the rules with redirection.

Chapter Six

Advanced Training Techniques

Expanding Commands and Cues

Once your Australian Shepherd has mastered basic obedience orders, continue developing their attentiveness by expanding to more advanced cues and signals. Their great working desire lets Aussies shine at a higher level of obedience.

Add Hand Signals - Associate each vocal command with a distinct hand signal. Point down for down, flat palm up for stay, sweeping hand motion for come, etc.

Increase Distance - Gradually step back as you offer orders, rewarding sustained prompt responses from increasing distances.

Proof in Distractions - With a long training lead on, practice commands outdoors around distractions like other dogs or in appealing locations like pet stores.

Vary settings - Raise requirements by rehearsing orders from all settings - backyard, front yard, wandering streetside, at the park, pet stores, etc.

Reward Speed! - Provide high-value goodies when your Aussie responds promptly to a cue. You desire snap reflexes. Use release cues freely.

Up the Duration - Increase how long your dog must obey instructions like stays, heel, and put. Randomly prolong times and change locales.

Weave Commands Together - After understanding individual signals, link together sequences of diverse commands like sit-stay-down-come-sit-stay. Keep it fun!

Use Real Life - Practice commands during real settings like a door opening, grasping the leash, while petting, when people approach, around food, etc.

Off-Leash Practice - In secure confined locations only, rehearse cues without the leash, rewarding outstanding responsiveness from a distance.

Advanced training gives crucial mental stimulation and reinforces control. Challenging your Australian Shepherd with higher requirements enhances your off-leash bond and handling skills.

Off-Leash Control

Well-trained Australian Shepherds can enjoy outstanding off-leash obedience due to their people-focused commitment. Use the following approaches to create reliable off-leash control:

Thorough On-Leash Skills - All commands should be rock solid on-leash with distractions before expecting off-leash compliance. Do not rush this fundamental work.

Secure Areas First - When first starting off-leash work, only practice in 100% secure enclosed spaces such as backyards with gates fastened and 6-foot fences.

Long Line Safety - Attach a 30-50 foot training lead to securely practice off-leash instructions at parks, trails, and open areas. Reel the pup back in if they ignore cues.

Always Reward Returns - When you call your pooch back, make it incredibly gratifying every time with super delectable food, play sessions, and loving praise. Coming must be fun!

Use Real prizes - Carry "jackpot" prizes like squirrel tails, dried liver, or tug toys reserved especially for off-leash recall success.

Increase Distraction Level - As reliability strengthens, purposely set up distractions like toys on the ground or individuals off in distance to prove focus.

Reinforce Consistently - Never let your Australian Shepherd ignore an instruction or lose attention. Keep them obediently engaged utilizing positive reinforcement.

Check-In Rewards - Periodically reward eye contact and checking in with you so they learn to continuously gaze back while off-leash roaming.

Emergency "Come" - Teach an emergency recall cue distinct from the usual "come" for those essential moments when you need an urgent off-leash response.

Have realistic expectations based on the environment and your dog's training fundamentals. An Australian Shepherd's innate tendency to keep you within sight helps boost off-leash reliability.

Agility and Trick Training

Smart, athletic Australian Shepherds thrive when trained for canine sports and activities. Two fantastic outlets for their energy and intellect are agility and recreational trick training.

Agility Foundations:

- Introduce equipment like tunnels, chutes, low jumps, teeters, wobble boards, fitness balls, etc. in backyards first.

- Shape confident behavior on each obstacle with treats - no pushing. Build drive by rewarding engagement.

- Cue obstacle names gleefully as your Aussie learns to enjoy negotiating each one.

- Link 2-3 obstacles together, use target sticks to guide direction and practice heel position between equipment.

- Focus on success and confidence-building in early training sessions. Increase difficulty progressively.

- Move to full agility course scenarios after mastering individual obstacles in low-distraction situations first.

Fun Tricks for Aussies:

- Spin, whirl, and circle are easy introductory tricks to shape. Lure and reward in incremental stages.

- Rolling over and playing dead come easy to many Aussies when hand indicated.

- Assign a "go find" cue for their abilities to search out and retrieve toys or hidden goodies.

- With a stable platform or object, educate them to place their feet up or hop on with a verbal cue.

- Shape them to run through tunnel or hoop-shaped props and to weave through legs or cones.

- Train them to catch sweets, discs, or balls flung in the air. Retrieving and catching creates confidence.

Keep training sessions brief, lively, and entertaining. Target training and clicker systems excel in teaching stunts and agility skills. Stay constructively motivated!

Chapter Seven

Common Behavioral Issues

Separation Anxiety

Separation anxiety is a typical concern in Australian Shepherds since they build close ties with their owners. Symptoms include frightened behavior, damage, and elimination when left alone. Use these preventative and treatment tips:

Prevention:

- Provide considerable socialization to foster independence and confidence in puppyhood. Introduce cautiously to alone time.

- Avoid continuously keeping your Aussie by your side the first few months. Enforced dependency on you makes separation tougher later.

- Establish a steady, predictable program with scheduled exercise, training, playing, and relaxing time.

- Give them a good 30-60 minute workout before each time they will be left alone. Tired pups cope better.

- Provide interactive food puzzles that dispense kibble while alone to equate being left with good things.

Treatment:

- Rule out or address any medical conditions like digestive difficulties that could be causing distress.

- Identify and gradually desensitize significant triggers like putting on shoes, and grabbing keys, towards relatively short absences.

- Use relaxing aids such as DAP diffusers, soothing caps, anxiety vests, and supplements if needed in extreme circumstances. Consult your vet.

- Teach an "all done" cue when you stop petting/playing that helps convey your disengagement. Reward calm behavior.

- Always keep returns low-key. Don't meet nervous, destructive conduct with calming attention. Wait for calm.

- Start with literally 5 seconds alone, encouraging calm conduct upon return, and then increase alone time very carefully over weeks/months.

- Provide interactive puzzle toys loaded with food when departing to serve as a positive diversion.

- Consult a trainer/behaviorist if severe. Medication may be necessary alongside training in some circumstances.

Patience, prevention, and desensitization are key when confronting an Aussie's separation difficulties. Medical assistance may be required alongside training for certain individuals.

Excessive Barking/Herding

Australian Shepherds were raised to bark and "herd" moving objects with their lips - therefore excessive barking at triggers or snappy, hyper behavior can develop without instruction. Here are methods to curb problem barking/herding:

Barking Deterrents:

- Use a "quiet" cue when they bark, praise quietness, and redirect to a toy or treat when they stop barking.

- Teach a mutually exclusive behavior like "go to mat" that prevents simultaneous problem barking by giving them an alternative activity.

- Desensitize to triggers like fence-running, passersby, and car sounds via gradual exposure from a distance mixed with redirection to toys or food puzzles.

- Avoid yelling, scaring, or over-stimulating your Aussie in response to barking – this might reinforce the tendency. Stay calmly neutral.

- White noise, vibration collars, and citronella spray collars can securely interrupt non stop barking so you can divert. Don't just suppress.

- Keep your Aussie exercised, enriched, and free of stress. Pups that get their physical and mental needs satisfied tend to bark less.

Curbing Herding/Nipping:

- Do not allow nipping or mouthing of people and teach an alternate activity like fetching a ball when stimulated.

- Redirect herding behavior onto appropriate chew toys. Use a tug toy to provide them an outlet to "win" against.

- If they nip or crowd kids, immediately give a time-out until settled. Firmly warn them "No herd".

- Avoid activities like fetch that provoke frenetic herding behaviors. Calm activities are preferable.

- Encourage relaxing behaviors like catching tranquil moments, stuffed Kongs, chewing bones, settle training, and relaxation techniques.

- Consider herding lessons to direct their impulses onto appropriate stock under a controlled atmosphere.

Be patient - barking and herding are intrinsic habits for Aussies, but you can teach them certain things are good outlets.

Digging/Chewing Destructiveness

Terrier-like digging or chewing damage is frequent in lively, often bored Australian Shepherd pups. Here are strategies to curb these damaging behaviors:

Digging Prevention:

- Provide adequate exercise, fun, training, and stimulation to prevent digs out of boredom.

- Offer a specific digging trench with buried toys/treats they are allowed to excavate. Reward digging there only.

- Try deterrents like burying their waste or adding unpleasant textures like pinecones at common dig spots.

- Block off or utilize an underground barrier to avoid digging beneath fences. Keep them supervised outdoors.

- Train an alternate behavior like "go to your bed" to transfer the digging urge onto an acceptable activity.

Curbing Chewing:

- Puppy-proof and remove all probable items they could chew on like shoes, furniture, clothing, kids' toys, etc. Set them up for success.

- Provide a wide selection of chew toys and rotate them periodically to keep them entertaining.

- Bitter anti-chew sprays deter chewing improper goods. Apply to furniture, baseboards, etc.

- Use flavor deterrents like cayenne pepper or citrus oil on goods.

- Keep pup monitored or crated when you can't watch attentively. Correct and divert any improper chewing promptly.

- Spend a focused hour working their brain and body before leaving them with chew toys. Prevent boredom-related chewing.

For both behaviors, the emphasis is on control and providing suitable outlets rather than just punishing the unpleasant conduct. With a lively working breed like the Aussie, an ounce of prevention is vital.

Chapter Eight

Nutrition and Exercise Needs

Dietary Requirements for Aussies

Australian Shepherds are energetic herding dogs with higher caloric needs than the usual pets. Feed quality food according to their life stage and energy level.

Puppy Diets:

- Feed a large breed puppy formula until at least 12-18 months old for controlled growth.

- Look for 25-30% protein, 12-15% fat, and calcium under 1.5% to help bone/joint development.

- 3-4 meals a day minimizes hunger-based negative behaviors.

Adult Diets:

- Feed adult food intended for high-energy dogs with 30% protein, and 20% fat once mature.

- Good proteins include meat, organ meat, and eggs. Avoid corn, wheat, soy, by-products.

- Moderate fat levels limit weight gain that strains joints. Omega fatty acids support coat health.

- Add glucosamine/chondroitin pills to enhance joint health and mobility.

Senior Diets:

- Reduce to 25% protein, 10-12% fat diet. Lower calorie density reduces weight gain.

- Increase fiber like pumpkin or vegetables to help digestion.

- Antioxidant-rich foods like berries, leafy greens, and fish oil maintain immune function.

- Monitor organ health with annual senior blood work at the vet.

Tips:

- Serve measured meals versus free feeding to prevent overeating.

- Keep fresh water available at all times. Limit exercise during heat waves.

- Adjust the amount provided based on the dog's weight, energy level, and metabolism.

- Discuss ideal nutritional needs with your veterinarian.

An Australian Shepherd's diet should maintain their high activity levels and metabolism. Tailor nutrition to keep your herding dog fit and healthy.

Establishing Feed Schedules

Australian Shepherds thrive on predictable routines with set meal times. Follow these ideas for an effective eating schedule:

Feed Multiple Small Meals

- Feed puppies 3-4 meals every day till 6-12 months old. Senior dogs are best with 2-3 meals as well.

- Most adult Aussies do best with 2 meals a day rather than 1 heavy meal.

Set the Schedule

- Feed close to the same times daily - for example, 7 am and 5 pm. Routines lessen anxiety.

- Avoid dining shortly before or after hard exercise or training. Wait 60-90 minutes.

- Feed frequently before excursions or hours alone to reduce boredom/stress chewing.

Measure Portions

- Determine appropriate calorie intake depending on the dog's age, size, and activity level.

- Weigh out the appropriate amount of food rather than eyeballing.

- Use measuring cups for uniformity versus letting the dog feast freely.

Stick to It

- Pick up uneaten food after 15-20 minutes until the next mealtime.

- Store surplus food sealed and out of reach to discourage snacking.

- Overfeeding leads to obesity which affects Aussie joints. Don't give in to begging.

Structured eating times and measured servings enhance health and make toilet schedules more regular. Aussies learn fast what to expect at mealtimes.

Importance of Daily Exercise and Mental Stimulation

As lively working dogs, Australian Shepherds require extensive daily physical and mental exercise to remain happy and well-adjusted. Make activity a priority every day.

Exercise Needs:

- A minimum of 30-60 minutes of intense activity like jogging, hiking, fetch, swimming, etc to reduce harmful tendencies.

- Aussies excel at dog sports like agility, dock diving, flying disc, herding competitions, and obedience that burn energy.

- Interactive play like tug of war and chasing balls tap into their herding background and inherent instincts.

- Take care not to over-exercise puppies until growth plates close to prevent joint injuries.

Mental Enrichment:

- Provide puzzle feeders and treat-stuffed chew toys to exercise their problem-solving skills.

- Rotate fresh toys to keep their smarts stimulated. Aussies grow bored easily.

- Train new commands, tricks, or behaviors every week. Attend group training programs for continual sociability and mental workouts.

- Let children chase sprinklers and water streams for mental and physical stimulation.

Preventing Boredom:

- Crate or confine unsupervised pups - they will get into mischief if left to roam bored and unattended.

- Aussies left alone outside in backyards are bored and destructive. They need family involvement.

- Returning home to walk and play with your Aussie on lunch breaks keeps the day interesting.

- Daycare, dog walkers or neighbors can help midday if your schedule necessitates protracted solitary confinement.

Working breed dogs like the Australian Shepherd require more than simply a stroll around the block. Make an activity plan to suit their needs every day.

Chapter Nine

Grooming and Health Care

Brushing and Bathing Basics

Frequent brushing and sometimes bathing keep an Australian Shepherd's coat clean, minimize shedding and enhance their natural oils. Follow these tips:

Shedding Control:

- Brush every day with an undercoat rake to remove loose hair and avoid matting.

- Use a slicker brush to loosen debris and distribute oils from the skin to coat tips.

- Bathe just 1-2 times a month. Over-bathing destroys coat oils.

- Increase brushing at peak seasonal shedding periods.

Bathing Best Practices:

- Bathe in warm (not hot) water using a light, hypoallergenic shampoo.

- Avoid getting water in your ears. Use cotton in ear canals.

- Rub shampoo down to the skin and rinse well to prevent irritation.

- Air dry properly or dry coat with a blow dryer on low heat to avoid chill.

Grooming Tools:

- Invest in an undercoat rake, slicker brush, comb, nail clippers, and ear cleaning.

- Introduce handling and brushing early to puppies following desensitization protocols.

- Keep sessions positive with praise. Hand-feed goodies as you groom.

- Correct tangles and mats ASAP before they tighten and pain. Never shave an Aussie coat.

Regular at-home brushing maintains your Aussie's coat neat in between professional grooming as needed for bathing and trim trimming. Make it a relaxing bonding ritual.

Nail Trimming and Dental Care

Consistent nail trims and tooth brushing contribute to general health and comfort for your Australian Shepherd. Implement these things early:

Nail Care:

- Trim nails regularly or bi-weekly depending on growth rate with clippers made for dogs.

- Introduce handling paws early. Give goodies as you briefly touch nails often to desensitize.

- Look for the pink fast and avoid clipping into it. Just trim the clear section.

- Use a nail file to gently soften rough edges if you trim too short.

- Apply styptic powder to stop bleeding if you accidently quick the nail.

Dental Care:

- Brush Aussie teeth 2-3 times a week using dog-friendly toothpaste.

- Use finger brushes or wraps that fit on your finger to rub the tooth surfaces.

- Give chews like raw bones, dental chews, and Frozen Kings. These behave like floss.

- Schedule annual veterinary dental cleanings as needed for tartar build-up.

- Monitor gums and teeth routinely for symptoms of infections that require antibiotics.

Preventive nail and dental care minimizes the incidence of infections and promotes comfort. Regularly handle paws and tongue from a young age so your Aussie welcomes grooming.

Vaccination and Vet Visit Schedules

To keep your Australian Shepherd healthy, adhere to the following vaccine and veterinary checkup schedule:

Puppy Vaccines:

- Initial set of core immunizations commencing at 6-8 weeks old, given every 2-4 weeks until 16-20 weeks old.

- Core vaccines include DA2P (distemper, adenovirus, parvovirus), and rabies vaccine.

- Optional: Leptospirosis, Lyme, and coronavirus vaccines depending on lifestyle and location concerns.

Adult Vaccines:

- Annual core vaccination boosts DA2P and rabies vaccine.

- Leptospirosis, Lyme, or coronavirus vaccines if previously prescribed.

- Senior dogs - see your vet regarding personalized immunization protocol. Potentially lesser dosages or titers.

Vet Visits:

- Monthly during puppyhood for physical exams, fecal tests, and heartworm prophylaxis.

- Annual wellness visit from age onward for a physical checkup with bloodwork, heartworm test, and parasite screen.

- Prompt vet exams for any indicators of disease such as vomiting, diarrhea, lameness, or injuries.

Prevention:

- Monthly heartworm, flea/tick, and gastrointestinal parasite prevention medicine.

- Spay/neuter by age 2 unless breeding on health clearances.

Routine wellness treatment prevents sickness and keeps your Aussie healthy and active long-term. Discuss your dog's immunization and visit schedule with your veterinarian.

Chapter Ten

The Joys of Living with an Australian Shepherd

Enjoying Your Fully-Trained Aussie

Life with an Australian Shepherd who has matured into a well-mannered, obedient companion is tremendously satisfying. Their adaptability makes them a great dog for many lifestyles.

Off-Leash Reliability:

- Hitting trails and tracks off-leash means adventure wherever you wander with an obedient Aussie by your side.

- Enjoy off-leash play at safe fenced parks, beaches, and open fields thanks to their recall training.

- Camping, trekking, and rural agricultural excursions become much more fun with your dog along for the walk.

Well-Mannered House Dog:

- No more jumping, pinching, or frantic behavior - just concentrated attention on you and proper indoor play.

- They wait respectfully at doors, settle comfortably for petting, and leave food alone until offered.

- Your Aussie now greets guests politely instead of bowling them over with zeal!

Trustworthy Family Dog:

- Parents may relax knowing their Aussie interacts nicely with kids following supervised socializing.

- They observe household norms and don't harass your cat or other pets. Peaceful multi-pet homes are conceivable.

- Car rides, meetings with friends, and public activities are more pleasant without unruly antics.

Living with a trained Australian Shepherd unleashes all the rewards of their intelligence, loyalty, and versatility. It requires labor but pays back tenfold!

Competing in Dog Sports

The athletic, determined Australian Shepherd excels at practically every dog sport. Some wonderful outlets for their energy include:

Agility - Weaving around obstacles, jumping hurdles, and scrambling up A-frames engages their bodies and wits. Aussies live for the challenge!

Flyball - This racing relay portrays their ball drive and swift feet to perfection. They explode off the box and rip down the lane with enthusiasm.

Dock Diving - Whether leaping nimbly off the dock after a bumper or pursuing their disc mid-air off the ramp, Aussies take to the air with ease.

Frisbee - Tireless disc chasers, Aussies will play catch until your arm wears out! Freestyle Frisbee performance shows off their fluid elegance and trainability.

Herding Trials - Get your Aussie's herding instincts revved up by doing what they were bred for by working sheep or ducks through an obstacle course.

Obedience/Rally Trials - They thrive executing concentrated heelwork, stays, retrieves, signals, and agility work with precision and enthusiasm among distracting trial environments.

Nosework - Following intricate smell trails to uncover buried "birch" taps into their olfactory talents and searching perseverance.

The focused teamwork, training, and joy of trialing or competing with your Aussie in their element is a particular bonding experience for any active owner.

Traveling and Adventuring with Your Dog

Australian Shepherds are wonderful adventure companions when properly trained for the road and trail. Travel tips:

Camping/Hiking - Acclimate to tent sleeping, bonfire sounds, and nature noises. Practice recall cues successfully off-leash. Keep well hydrated and bring dog first aid kits.

Road Trips – Accustomed to car driving from puppyhood. Use crates and canine seat belts. Plan pet-friendly stops. Never leave dogs alone in hot vehicles.

Dog-Friendly Lodging - Research ahead of time. National brands like La Quinta, Motel 6, and Red Roof Inn commonly accept dogs. Avoid leaving alone unless thoroughly crate trained.

Dog Sport Trialing - Book pet-friendly hotels in advance that waive costs. Crate or confine when departing to prevent noise disturbances. Bring cleaning supplies.

Flying with Dogs - Get them acquainted with crates & carriers. Check airline requirements. Consider a pet moving service for less hassle. Attach ID tags at all times.

Public Manners – Practice loose leash walking, ignoring distractions, and greeting strangers properly before public excursions. Set a good example!

Match the journey to your specific dog's training fundamentals and temperament. Ensuring your Australian Shepherd has a dependable recall, etiquette with unfamiliar dogs, and confinement training enhances the options. Travel safely!

20 homemade food dish ideas for Australian Shepherds with ingredients and preparation instructions

1. Chicken with Rice

Ingredients:

- 2 cups cooked chicken, shredded

- 1 cup cooked brown rice

- 1 cup carrots, shredded

- 2 tbsp olive oil

- 1 tsp garlic powder

Instructions:

Combine all ingredients in a bowl. Portion into individual servings and put in the freezer. Thaw before feeding. Provides protein and fiber.

2. Beef and Sweet Potato

Ingredients:
- 1 lb lean ground beef
- 2 sweet potatoes, boiled and mashed
- 1 cup green beans, diced
- 2 eggs
- 2 tbsp coconut oil

Instructions:
Cook beef completely, and drain fat. Mix with remaining ingredients. Portion into servings and chill for up to 5 days or freeze. Provides antioxidants.

3. Pumpkin with Peanut Butter

Ingredients:

- 1 cup pure pumpkin puree

- 1/4 cup natural peanut butter

- 1/2 cup Greek yogurt

- 1 cup whole wheat flour

- 1 egg

Instructions:

Whisk together items until well blended. Pour the mixture into a greased baking dish. Bake at 350°F for 30 minutes. Cut into bars and serve. Provides fiber.

4. Chicken Liver Training Treats

Ingredients:

- 1 pound chicken livers

- 1 cup flour

- 2 eggs, beaten

- 1/2 cup breadcrumbs

Instructions:

Coat livers with flour, dip in eggs, then coat in breadcrumbs. Bake at 400°F for 15 minutes until cooked through. Cut into small pieces. Provides protein.

5. Frozen Yogurt Bark

Ingredients:
- 2 cups plain Greek yogurt
- 1 banana, mashed
- 1/2 cup blueberries
- 2 tbsp honey

Instructions:
Mix yogurt, banana, blueberries, and honey. Spread onto a parchment-lined baking sheet. Freeze for 2-3 hours until stiff. Break into pieces to serve. Provides calcium.

6. Chicken and Vegetable Soup

Ingredients:

- 2 boneless, skinless chicken breasts

- 3 carrots, chopped

- 2 celery stalks, diced

- 1 zucchini, chopped

- 4 cups chicken broth

- 1/4 cup rice

Instructions:

Combine all ingredients in a saucepan. Simmer until chicken is done and rice is soft for about 30 minutes. Shred chicken before serving. Provides vitamin A.

7. Apple Cinnamon Oatmeal

Ingredients:

- 1 cup rolled oats

- 1 apple, chopped

- 1 tbsp peanut butter

- 1 tsp cinnamon

- 1 cup water

Instructions:

Combine all ingredients in a pot and simmer over medium heat until thickened about 5 minutes. Let cool before serving. Provides fiber.

8. Sweet Potato Chews

Ingredients:

- 2 sweet potatoes, peeled and sliced
- 1/2 cup pumpkin puree
- 1 egg
- 1 tsp cinnamon

Instructions:

Preheat the oven to 325°F. Mix all ingredients together. Spread onto a greased baking sheet. Bake for 35 minutes until dry and chewy. Provides vitamin C.

9. Banana Peanut Butter Pops

Ingredients:

- 2 ripe bananas, peeled and chopped
- 1/4 cup peanut butter
- 1/4 cup Greek yogurt

Instructions:

Mash bananas with a fork. Mix in peanut butter and yogurt. Pour into popsicle molds and freeze overnight. Provides potassium.

10. Veggie Scramble

Ingredients:
- 2 eggs, beaten
- 1/2 cup spinach, chopped
- 1/4 cup red bell pepper, diced
- 2 tbsp feta cheese
- 1 tbsp coconut oil

Instructions:

Heat coconut oil in a pan over medium heat. Add egg mixture and veggies. Cook, scrambling often until eggs are set. Top with feta before serving. Provides vitamin K.

11. Salmon and Sweet Potato

Ingredients:
- 8 ounces cooked salmon, flakes
- 1 cooked sweet potato, mashed
- 1 tbsp olive oil
- 1/4 cup green beans
- 1 hard-boiled egg, diced

Instructions:
Mix together salmon, sweet potato, olive oil, green beans, and egg. Portion into individual servings and refrigerate for up to 4 days. Provides omega-3s.

12. Pumpkin Peanut Butter Dog Biscuits

Ingredients:
- 2 1/2 cups whole wheat flour
- 1/2 cup pumpkin puree

- 1/4 cup peanut butter

- 1 egg

- 1 tbsp cinnamon

Instructions:

Preheat the oven to 350°F. Mix together all ingredients into a dough. Roll out dough and cut into shapes using cookie cutters. Bake for 30 minutes until firm. Provides fiber.

13. Beef Liver Brownies

Ingredients:

- 1 lb beef liver, cooked

- 1 1/2 cups oats

- 1 egg - 1 banana, mashed

- 1 tbsp coconut oil

Instructions:

Blend all ingredients in a food processor until smooth. Pour into a baking pan. Refrigerate 1 hour until hard. Cut into squares. Provides iron.

14. Frozen Coconut Berry Treats

Ingredients:

- 1 cup coconut milk

- 1 cup blueberries

- 1 banana, sliced

- 1 tbsp honey

Instructions:

Blend together coconut milk, blueberries, banana, and honey. Pour into popsicle molds and freeze overnight. Provides antioxidants.

15. Peanut Butter Apple Dog Treats

Ingredients:

- 1 apple, chopped

- 1/4 cup peanut butter

- 1 tbsp honey

- 1 egg

- 1 cup whole wheat flour

- 1/2 tsp cinnamon

Instructions:

Preheat the oven to 350°F. Mix together ingredients into a dough. Roll out and cut into shapes with cookie cutters. Bake for 15 minutes. Let cool before serving. Provides fiber.

16. Carob Peanut Butter Pup-sicles

Ingredients:
- 1 banana, sliced
- 2 tbsp peanut butter
- 1 tbsp carob powder
- 1/4 cup Greek yogurt

Instructions:

Blend all ingredients together until smooth. Pour into popsicle molds and freeze overnight. Insert sticks before serving. Provides potassium.

17. Beef Barley Stew

Ingredients:

- 1/2 pound lean beef, diced

- 3 carrots, chopped

- 2 celery stalks, chopped

- 1/2 cup barley

- 4 cups beef broth

Instructions:

Combine all ingredients in a saucepan. Bring to a boil, then reduce heat and simmer for 30 minutes until beef and barley are cooked through. Provides niacin.

18. Pumpkin Pie Puppy Pancakes

Ingredients:

- 1 mashed banana

- 1/2 cup canned pumpkin

- 2 eggs

- 1/2 cup oats

- 1 tsp cinnamon

Instructions:

Mix all ingredients together until blended thoroughly. Scoop batter onto an oiled griddle. Cook over medium heat for 2-3 minutes per side until browned. Provides vitamin A.

19. Frozen Berry Yogurt Bars

Ingredients:
- 1 cup Greek yogurt
- 1 cup blueberries
- 1 banana, mashed
- 1 tbsp honey

Instructions:
Blend together all ingredients. Spread equally onto a parchment-lined baking sheet. Freeze for 2 hours until stiff. Cut into bars before serving. Provides antioxidants.

20. Cheesy Chicken with Rice

Ingredients:

- 2 cups cooked chicken, shredded

- 1 1/2 cups brown rice, cooked

- 1/4 cup cheddar cheese, shredded

- 1 tbsp olive oil

- 1 tsp garlic powder

Instructions:

Mix all ingredients together. Portion into servings and chill for up to one week or freeze. Provides protein and probiotics.